COLOSSIANS

ALIVE IN CHRIST

10 Publishing
a division of 10 of those.com

First published in Great Britain in 2016

British Library Cataloguing in Publication Data
A record for this book is available from the British Library

ISBN: 978-1-910587-75-1
Designed by Diane Warnes
Printed in the UK

10Publishing, a division of 10ofthose.com
Unit C, Tomlinson Road, Leyland, PR25 2DY, England
Email: info@10ofthose.com
Website: www.10ofthose.com

Andy Mason

24 UNDATED DEVOTIONS
THROUGH THE BOOK OF COLOSSIANS

DAY 1

READ Colossians 1:1–2

Paul starts Colossians with his normal greeting, but this is not just an ordinary 'Hello'! Rather, it's packed, as always, with big thoughts about God and the local church.

In verse 1, we're reminded that the letter to the Colossians isn't a few quick spiritual thoughts from a Christian leader, but it's an authoritative letter. It has the authority of an apostle. The word 'apostle' originally meant someone who was 'sent out' on the authority of another – in this case Jesus Christ himself! To listen to Paul the apostle, then, is to listen to Jesus Christ speaking, which is itself undergirded by the will of God. This is the reason that the New Testament local church was devoted to the teaching of the apostles (cf. Acts 2:42; 4:33), which, in turn, is a pattern for us as well. Final authority in any church resides not in pastors or denominations, but in the authoritative teaching of the apostles – preserved for us in Scripture.

In verse 2, we're given a vision of what the local church is. Of course, our day-to-day experience of the local church may go up and down, and be more or less encouraging at different times. But here we're taught to look at our local church through the lens of what God has made it. According to this verse, the local church is a community of people:

- who are named by their relationship with Christ ('in Christ')
- who are defined by God as blameless and set apart ('holy')
- who live their lives by faith ('faithful')
- who have been made into a family ('brothers')

Wow! What a community to be a part of!

Lastly, at the end of verse 2, Paul reminds us of the Father's great blessing given to every local church: grace and peace. These summarise the great blessings of the gospel. The Father's grace and peace are enough for all the sins, shortcomings and failures of his church.

REFLECTION

1. What's encouraging about the Bible being the final authority in the local church?

2. Do you look at your local church from God's perspective?

3. How do you see the Father's grace and peace at work in your church?

DAY 2

READ Colossians 1:3–8

Spiritual leaders must pray. We see that all through the Bible with prophets, priests and kings, and Paul has definitely learnt that lesson as well. These verses, as do all Paul's letters, show us a man who prays. The thing that's excited Paul here, and caused him to thank God, is the church's faith, hope and love. In his mind, this is the inevitable impact the gospel makes in any believer or church. Faith, hope and love are the vital signs of the gospel's power working in our lives. Paul's great concern in this letter is that the Colossians hold on to this gospel – and so keep on living in faith, hope and love.

'Remember the gospel of Christ!' Paul is effectively saying in verses 5–6. This gospel holds out a real and powerful future hope to a world without any hope. In 1:27, we read that it is nothing less than Jesus Christ himself and the glory that we get with him. This hope-filled gospel is initially likened to a powerful life-giving seed that produces transforming effects in our lives – and 'All over the world' (v. 6). The good news about Christ isn't useless or weak, but it has life-giving power and gives hope across the whole world. We need to hold on to this gospel tightly.

According to verse 7, the good news had come to the Colossians not from Paul but from Epaphras. Here we get a good description of what their gospel minister is like. He is:

- 'our dear fellow-servant' – leaders are called to serve people (a closer translation is in fact 'slave') and not to exalt themselves
- 'faithful' – leaders are called to have long-term stickability and commitment
- a 'minister of Christ' – leaders are to be committed to the cause of Christ, and not to be distracted from him

We need to be thankful for committed leaders like this who have brought us the life-giving gospel of Jesus Christ. Let's not take them for granted!

REFLECTION

1. How is your faith, hope and love at the moment?

2. What impact has the gospel had in individual believers that you know?

3. Think of a leader who has been faithful to you and give God thanks for them.

DAY 3

READ Colossians 1:9–10

In 1:3 we're told that Paul prays for the Colossians, and here in these verses we're told how and what Paul actually prays for them. Firstly, he has confidence when he prays for them because of all that he has heard about them (v. 9) – the gospel's power has already been working in them to produce faith, hope and love. Notice how Paul prays for them not because they're not bearing fruit, but because they are bearing fruit. That spurs him on in confident praying!

Secondly, we can learn a lot here for our prayer lives from what Paul prioritises in his prayers for the believers in Colossae. His continual prayer has been full of requests that they might be filled with the knowledge of God's will (v. 9; see also 2:9–10). We might be tempted to think that this is about prayer for their guidance in specific situations of life, but actually it's bigger than that. It's about grasping how central Jesus Christ is in God's plan (look ahead to 1:15–20; 2:2–3 and Eph. 1:9–10). Wisdom and understanding here are really about knowing God's plan for the world – which is, in essence, to put everything under Jesus Christ. Here's a new priority for our prayer lives: to get a good understanding of God's plans to exalt Christ over the whole world!

The result of this knowledge of Christ is a changed life (v. 10). Knowing Christ always brings practical changes to how we live. The changed life is described in a number of ways as a worthy life, pleasing Christ, bearing fruit (cf. 1:6) and increasing in the knowledge of God. This is what we're moving towards as a result of knowing Christ. So, if you want to see your life changed, keep asking God to show you how important Jesus Christ is. As we get a bigger grasp of who he is, changes will inevitably result in our day-to-day living.

REFLECTION

1. What are the things you really long for and desire at the moment? What has been filling your prayers?

2. How would you summarise God's purposes through Christ (Eph. 1:9–10)?

DAY 4

READ Colossians 1:11–14

There are obviously seasons when believers and churches become dry, weary and fed up. There are times when our faith feels weak and our future spiritual state might look a bit shaky. It may be a mild comfort, then, to know that this is nothing new! Paul is praying here for the Colossian church that they might have power. Presumably, he only prays that because he knows how weak and wavering they might have become. We need this prayer as well – to be 'strengthened with all power' from God's might (v. 11). Realistically, how can we survive without it? How can your church survive without it? This is how we get the endurance, patience, joy and gratitude Paul is talking about (vv. 11–12). These qualities aren't in-built into us and they're not easy things to keep hold of in a discouraging world. We need God's power to be happy, grateful believers, and to get power, we have to pray!

As Paul prays in verse 12, he can't help but look up to how God has saved us. Paul is a deeply thankful man. He knows that the only reason we can stand as one of God's people is God's work for us. Notice that God is the one doing everything here in these verses. He has 'qualified', 'delivered' and 'transferred' (vv. 12–13, ESV) us. In other words, you and I haven't earned our spiritual qualifications, or delivered ourselves, or signed up for a transfer, but it's all God's work from start to finish.

This work, though, is always done through Jesus Christ (vv. 13–14). A new kingdom life, liberation and forgiveness are yours today because God has rescued you through his much-loved Son. Christ is the magnet that Paul keeps being drawn back to because all of God's blessings come through him.

REFLECTION

1. What kind of strength or power do you need to pray for today? Are there others who are weak who need your prayers?

2. What difference does it make to your discipleship that it's the Father who has saved you, and not you?

3. What does life in the kingdom of the Son look like?

DAY 5

READ Colossians 1:15–20

We saw yesterday how Christ is like a magnet for Paul – he is always drawn back to him. That 'magnetic effect' becomes very clear in these verses. Paul, in thinking about what the Father has done for his people in verses 12–13, now helps the Colossians (and us) to see who Christ really is. This is a key passage in the letter, and in the whole Bible, because it focuses us on the absolute centrality of Jesus Christ in everything. The Colossians (and we too) need to be constantly reminded that the Christian life is Christ.

These verses are jam-packed with great things about Christ, but the big idea going through them is Christ's supremacy over everything. We read that:

- all things have been made by him (v. 16)
- all things were created for him (v. 16)
- he is before all things (v. 17)
- in him all things hold together (v. 17)
- he is pre-eminent in everything (v. 18)
- all of God's fullness is in him (v. 19)
- all things are reconciled through him (v. 20)

Christ is clearly supreme over all – whether its supernovas, seagulls, sandstorms, spiritual forces or science. It has all been made for him and finds its proper end in him. In fact, we might say that if we don't understand Christ, we don't really understand anything in the world around us. We're left in the dark and can only be confused about what our world is all about. But, from these verses, we can see that all the details of our life find their goal in him. We have been made by him, through him and for him.

REFLECTION

1. To what extent does the world around you acknowledge Christ? What does that tell you about the world?

2. Are there areas of your life that aren't related to Christ?

3. Given that God's fullness has been given to Christ (v. 19), how should we treat Christ?

DAY 6

READ Colossians 1:15–20

Yesterday we thought about the supremacy of Christ from these verses. We were reminded that the Christian life is Christ.

Today we will see that everything in heaven and on earth is related to Christ and can only be understood through him. He is like the hub of a wheel, and everything else is like the spokes of the wheel, finding their end in him. This is why Jesus Christ is the one who reconciles all things to God (v. 20). Everything has been made for him and he holds everything together. Therefore, when the world goes wrong, only he can fix everything and reconcile everything to God. The world belongs to Jesus Christ and is for him alone, and so he is the only one who can make peace between God and the world. Only Jesus could die on the cross to make us right with God (v. 20). There can be no other mediator for the world because the world doesn't belong to anyone else. Jesus is Supreme, and therefore he alone is the Saviour.

Jesus Christ's supremacy in all things, and his death on the cross, mean that only he can be the supreme head of the church (v. 18). That's why no monarch, pope nor pastor can claim authority over God's church. Christ alone is the head, the beginning and the firstborn Son over God's church. He alone is pre-eminent. It's surprising how this simple and obvious truth can be marginalised or forgotten by both churches and their leaders. When this happens, churches inevitably move towards authoritarian leadership, false teaching and spiritual chaos. Let's not just give lip service to Christ's supremacy, but let's uphold it in our practice and attitudes. Christ is always supreme over God's people.

REFLECTION

1. *Why can only Jesus alone be the Saviour of the world?*
2. *If we forget that Jesus is the head over God's church, what kind of things start to happen?*
3. *How does it change Christianity if we say that Jesus was only a prophet who taught us God's word?*

DAY 7

READ Colossians 1:21–23

The shocking message of these verses is that a relationship with God isn't natural to us. In fact, we're told here that it's never been something that we naturally want or desire. Verse 21 tells us that, by nature, we're alienated, hostile to God and given over to sin. No one naturally has a relationship with God.

This natural opposition to God is never changed through us 'recognising the error of our ways' or 'making amends'. Rather, our opposition can only be healed by God himself: he reconciles us to himself through his Son (v. 22). In other words, we can't reconcile ourselves to God, but *only God can reconcile us to God.* And this is what he has done through his Son. Amazingly, the reconciliation that we now enjoy isn't just the end of hostilities, but it's also a totally new position and identity. We have now become holy, blameless and above reproach (v. 22) through Jesus' death on the cross.

Yet, this reconciliation is even bigger than us personally being made right with God, for we see that Christ reconciles *all* things to God. The gospel isn't the hope just that we personally will be saved, but that our fallen world itself will one day be remade and put right with God. There is a hope of a new creation. What a great hope our world has! Though, in rejoicing in this, we should guard against those who teach that every individual will therefore automatically be made right through Jesus (an idea called universalism). Verse 23 makes clear that this cannot be the case, as reconciliation only occurs as we persevere in faith in the Son. Without explicitly trusting in and following Jesus, we won't get to be a part of this fantastic plan God has for the world.

REFLECTION

1. What, according to this passage, is the basis of your relationship with God? How do you know that you're secure with God?

2. What things will help you continue in unwavering faith in the hope of the gospel (v. 23)?

DAY 8

READ Colossians 1:24–29

Even if we're not pastors or full-time Christian workers, it's good to know what their job description should be because that helps us understand what the church should be. Here Paul describes what his ministry is all about:

- God has given him the job of making his word known (v. 25)
- this word is called 'the mystery' that's been revealed (v. 26)
- this 'mystery' is summed up as 'Christ in you' (v. 27)

Paul's job description is, therefore, about making Jesus Christ known through the preaching of the word, with the end goal that believers might become mature in their relationship with Christ (v. 28). Paul's whole life is given over to this goal (v. 29) of the church's fullness in Christ, and he's willing to suffer anything for it. Indeed, in verse 24 he sees his own ministry as a continuation of Christ's own suffering ministry.

This is the job description of every spiritual leader, even if their precise roles differ. They're not chairmen of a social club, but their call is to make Christ known. God has called them to proclaim the gospel, warn and teach his people. They are to strive for the maturity of the church in Christ – and even to be willing to suffer for that goal.

So, thank God for your leaders, pray for them and encourage them in this role because it'll be very hard for you to become mature in Christ without them. And make sure that you yourself are aligned with this scriptural goal for the church. Remember that your local church isn't any member's private possession, but it's about Christ and growing into him. This is what every member is called to strive for, whether they're leaders or not.

REFLECTION

1. How have you been thinking about or treating the leaders in your church? Is your thinking aligned with Paul's job description here?

2. How can you join in this battle for the church's maturity in Christ? What can you contribute?

DAY 9

READ Colossians 2:1–5

What's your life about today? What's your mind focused on at the moment? What are you passionate about? In these verses, the apostle Paul opens up his heart to us and shows us what his life is about. We've already seen from 1:24–29 that his focus in ministry has been Jesus Christ, which has meant suffering (v. 24) and hard work (v. 29). Now, he speaks more about his great 'struggle' in ministry. We learn from Paul here about how to use our lives well.

We see that all his effort has gone into pushing the churches in Colossae and Laodicea towards a deeper knowledge of Christ (2:1). This is because he trusts that true understanding, knowledge and wisdom are all centred on Jesus Christ (vv. 2–3; see also 1:15–20). He longs for the churches to have a 'full' understanding and knowledge of Christ. This is what drives his ministry and his letter-writing to the Colossians in the first place. At the centre of Paul's passion is Christ.

We must, therefore, beware of anything that might diminish or de-prioritise Christ in our lives. Paul himself warns about the 'plausible arguments' from some (v. 4, ESV) that might impact the believers' Christ-centredness. Heeding this warning, we must, accordingly, struggle to keep our lives focused on Christ. We need to remind ourselves that a life centred on anything else is wasted and foolish, and not let ourselves be distracted or pulled away by the 'plausible arguments' of others. Let's aspire towards the firmness of faith in Christ mentioned in verse 5. Surely, we want this to be a description of our spiritual state, and our church as well? Let your life today be shaped by this passion.

REFLECTION

1. Have you been drawn away from Christ by anything, or are you using your energy on Christ – both for yourself and others?

2. Can you think of any 'plausible arguments' used, inside or outside the church, that might draw us away from Christ?

These verses are key verses in the whole letter and summarise, in many ways, the main teaching of Colossians. Paul's big point here is that the Christian life, as it is lived, isn't different from the Christian life as it is received. He wants the church to remain rooted in Jesus Christ, and not drift away to something else.

Paul's encouragement to the church in verse 6 is, therefore, to walk in Christ 'as you received Christ' and 'as you were taught'. In other words, there's nothing more to add to the Christ who they first put their faith in and started to follow. He's the same complete Saviour we have always known. As a consequence, we don't start with Christ and then move on to 'bigger and better things'. Christ is always the bigger and better thing we need! People sometimes want to add special teachings, people or experiences to Jesus Christ. They maintain that we need these in order to be truly 'spiritual'. But these verses (and the whole of Colossians) make clear that simply being in Christ is always enough. What we really need is the same Christ we received in the past.

Of course, none of this means, though, that we don't grow or mature as believers. In 1:28 we have already read of how Paul is working for the church's maturity. Paul isn't calling the believers to passivity or spiritual laziness, but to an active walking in Christ. This means being 'rooted and built up in him' (v. 7). So, while believers should be 'established' in the faith, they are still to grow up into Christ. This growth is steady, stable and active. Accordingly, we don't need to run after fads, but, rather, we can look to be built up in the same Christ whom we have always known.

REFLECTION

1. Can you think of any things that people sometimes want to add to Christ? Why don't we need these things?

2. In what ways do you need to grow up in Christ?

3. At the end of verse 7 Paul calls us to abound in thanksgiving (ESV). What do you have to be thankful for?

DAY 11

READ Colossians 2:8–15

Paul has already warned the Colossians about 'plausible arguments' (2:4, ESV), and here he warns them further about being captured by lies and false wisdom (v. 8). It seems there was a kind of popular, but false and worldly, spirituality that might be in danger of deceiving them. None of us should ever think that we're invulnerable to such deception. How easy it is to be led astray and fascinated by some new movement or message that subtly draws us away from Christ! It's important, therefore, for us to hear the warning of these verses.

Paul wants us to keep our eyes on Christ and so he deliberately lifts our gaze to him and reminds us that:

- all the fullness of God is found in Christ (v. 9)
- we have been filled with God himself in Christ (v. 10)
- we have died and been raised to a new life with Christ (vv. 11–12)
- our hearts have been circumcised in Christ for a new beginning with God (v. 13)
- our sins have been dealt with at the cross (v. 14)
- every spiritual authority and power lays defeated at Christ's feet (v. 15)

We're much less likely to drift from Christ if our mind and heart are filled with these truths. On the other hand, we're much more prone to be captured by 'hollow and deceptive philosophy' (v. 8) when we feel that Christ is small, unimportant and weak. We only add to Christ when we feel that Christ is not very much to begin with. Therefore, it's crucial that we remind ourselves constantly of the greatness of Christ and all that he is for us. Believers and churches will only stand in Christ when they're filled with Christ and all that he's done for them.

REFLECTION

1. Why might we become fascinated by new movements or teachings that subtly marginalise Christ?

2. What, according to these verses, is so great about knowing Jesus Christ?

DAY 12

READ Colossians 2:16–23

The trappings of outward religion such as buildings, ceremonies, clothing, festivals and rules can make people feel spiritual. They help people to know where to go, what to do and when to do it. This is why the world's religions are full of such things. However, Paul makes clear here: be wary of them! They have nothing to do with life in Jesus Christ (v. 16). Even if the Old Testament made such things necessary for a season, they were only shadows of things to come (v. 17). The only thing that matters now is Christ (v. 17). Beware, then, of becoming focused on the outward trappings and organisational details of your local church! The one thing that really matters is Christ.

Be wary too of another form of religion: the reported experiences of self-important spiritual leaders (v. 18). Some will boast of what God has told them or showed them, and may even speak about angelic visitations. This can have a seductive power and draw crowds, but in reality these very leaders may themselves have drifted from Christ as their experiences have subtly started to replace Christ as the centre of their faith.

The shocking message here is that all forms of religion are, without Christ, worldly (v. 22). They may seem spiritual but they don't really deal with sin (v. 23) and can only give us superficial rules – 'Do not handle! Do not taste! Do not touch!' (v. 21). A Christ-filled life, though, is a new life that no longer belongs to the things of this world (v. 20). It's a life that has died and been raised with Christ (see 2:12) and now reigns with him. It's a life built not upon man's self-made religion but on Christ alone. In summary, don't run after man's religion, but, rather, get life from Christ.

REFLECTION

1. What trappings of religion have you seen in your experience? How can these things replace Christ?

2. Why won't man-made rules and regulations deal with the problem of sin? What deals with the problem of sin?

DAY 13

READ Colossians 3:1–4

As believers we have two lives: an *outward* life and a *secret* life. The outward life is our life in this world – our relationships, our jobs, our circumstances. This is what people call our 'normal' life. The secret life, though, is what we have through Jesus Christ (v. 3). It's a secret life because it's hidden and invisible at the moment, but it's the life we get through being united to Christ. (The phrase 'with Christ' is mentioned twice in these verses.) In fact, we're so closely united to him that Paul can say that we've died and been raised with Christ (v. 3 and v. 1). We've become new people with a new life. Our outward, 'normal' life will one day come to an end, but our secret life with Christ will go on forever. The full glory of this secret life will be revealed when Jesus comes back (v. 4).

Given that we have this new, secret life, Paul commands us to seek it and set our minds on it (vv. 1–2). Notice how realistic he is about us – he knows that the concerns of our outward lives tend to crowd out the hidden life we have in Christ. Amazing as our privileges are, there are a thousand distractions, subtle comforts and sins that pull us away from him. So, we must be disciplined to seek this life and focus our minds on it. The original wording points to this being a regular, ongoing thing. We must *continually* seek the life above with Jesus Christ, or we'll be drawn away.

The Scripture is saying to us here: be what you have become in Christ! You've gained a new life, now live that out. You've been raised, so think about where you belong. Let your life today be shaped not by your circumstances or the opinions of others but by your hidden life in Christ.

REFLECTION

1. How does your new life in Christ reshape how you look at your outward life?

2. Are there any routines or habits you could develop that might help you to refocus regularly on the life that you have in Christ?

DAY 14

READ Colossians 3:5–7

Yesterday we looked at the reality of our new, hidden life in Christ. This big perspective shapes the rest of what is said in this chapter. Everything in our lives is affected by this massive change in who we are. We are now, as individuals and as churches, called to live out a new life in Jesus Christ.

Verse 5 makes it clear that we can't both have life in Christ and life in sin. Consequently, we're called not to negotiate or procrastinate with sin in our lives but to kill and eradicate it. Our life in Christ leads us, in other words, to take drastic action with sin. The word 'earthly' here is not referring to physical things, as if our bodies are in and of themselves bad, but to a fallen world. This is contrasted with the heavenly life we have with Christ (see 3:1).

The particular sins Paul focuses on in verse 5 are out-of-control sex and out-of-control desires. Notice how he traces this all back to idol worship at the end of the verse. When we replace the living God with false gods, our lives spin out of control into all kinds of sexual sins and addictions. Paul reminds us in verse 6 that these things don't bring life, but God's just anger.

Life in Christ, on the other hand, brings a completely different mindset. Instead of idols, sexual immorality and addictions, we now have Christ, and so we now seek to live his way (in contrast to the old way, v. 7). The old ways belong to our past and have no place in our future. As people in Christ, we don't negotiate or procrastinate with immorality and addiction, but we kill it, knowing that we've been called to a new heavenly life in Jesus.

REFLECTION

1. Are there any obvious outward expressions of sexual immorality in your life today? Are there secret desires or lusts that you're cultivating?

2. Why do these things not fit with life in Christ?

3. How will you put these things to death?

DAY 15

READ Colossians 3:8–10

In these verses Paul is continuing to think about the practical implications of this new life in Christ and how it changes us. He's already spoken of the new mindset we're to have (3:1–4). In verses 9–10 he speaks of the big change in terms of an old 'me' and a new 'me'. Our old selves were shaped by certain 'practices' (see v. 5), but these practices no longer belong to the new person we have now 'put on' in Christ. A big change has occurred: we have become new people who are being remade in the image of Christ (v. 10). It's like we've emigrated to a new country and now we take on the language and habits of our new home. We're citizens of a different nation – and live accordingly.

All this has a very practical outworking in our relationships. The way we deal with other people is massively changed according to verse 8. Temper tantrums, harsh and unkind words, hatred and obscenities have no place in the Christian life. This isn't about developing some public spotless image, but about deep change in my friendships, family, marriage and dealings with people in the workplace. The new self produces new words and new relationships.

Notice as well the specific impact on truth-telling (v. 9). Of course, it makes perfect sense that Christ, who is himself Truth, should have a truth-telling people. It's surprising, therefore, how much deceit, misleading words and political games can mark local churches. Sometimes we're so eager to get our way that we can compromise honesty and openness. In those moments, though, we're starting to live outside of Christ and we're undoing what God has done amongst us.

REFLECTION

1. How would you like your relationships to be shaped by the presence of Christ in you? How can you work towards that?

2. When are you most tempted to tell lies/ adjust the truth? How does being in Christ change the fear or pride that lies behind your lying?

DAY 16

READ Colossians 3:11

What a vision this verse gives us of the local church! Paul has been helping the Colossians to see what it means to be people in Christ and the impact that has on their lives. Yesterday in verses 9–10 we thought about the new self we have 'put on' as believers. Here in verse 11, though, we see that this new self isn't just something that happens to individuals, but it's something that applies to the whole church. We're a new people in Jesus Christ.

All of us come into the local church with different backgrounds, experiences and gifts. Some are rich, others are poor; some are black, others are Asian; some are university-educated, others left school at sixteen. Yet, Paul says, none of these backgrounds define us when we're gathered as church. The huge religious, cultural and social differences of that time (for example between Jew and Gentile, or slaves and free men) were no longer to mean anything for the Colossians, and the same applies to us today. The local church is a community that makes every man-made difference unimportant.

The local church is like this, not because we're simply 'into equality', but because we're Christ's people. He's absolute and what he has done at the cross is final, and so every other marker of who we are has been made, relative to him, unimportant. The one thing that truly matters in the local church is Christ. He 'is all, and is in all' (v. 11). And we show that we take this seriously by minimising every other kind of man-made division and difference. Ultimately, Christ is glorified and honoured by our unity in the middle of many differences – because we define ourselves by him alone. This is a powerful vision for every local church community.

REFLECTION

1. Through which categories do you view the people in your local church? What's the most significant for you in the way you view them?

2. How can we promote this 'Christ is all, and is in all' thinking in our local churches?

DAY 17

READ Colossians 3:12–14

A lot of the change Paul has been speaking about in this chapter so far has been *negative*. That is, his emphasis has been on killing our old life before Christ, and therefore what we, as believers, need to 'put off'. In these verses, Paul now speaks about the *positive* change new life in Christ produces in us. He speaks here of what we need to 'put on'.

Again, we see that change starts with what we have already become in Christ – a loved, chosen and holy people (v. 12). We are now called to live this out in the details of our lives. For example, knowing that we've already been declared holy in Christ should motivate us to actually seek holiness in our lives, or knowing that we're chosen to become like Christ ought to drive us to change.

Notice the specific nature of the list of qualities in verses 12–13. The change produced in us is not vague or general, but leads to specific and practical traits in us – compassion, kindness, humility, gentleness, patience and forgiveness. These qualities are basically all about love (v. 14), which is the hallmark of the Christian life (see Rom. 13:9; Gal. 5:14). Spiritual maturity always displays itself in changed relationships. Who we are with other people reveals who we are with Christ.

Our role in the change process outlined here is to *put* these things on. Observe that, even though Christ's life is the power to change us, Paul calls us to effort, work and discipline in becoming loving people. We are to act in the middle of our relationships and take responsibility for our spiritual growth. As we do that, God will work in us. A living faith in Christ always shows itself in the kind of love that Christ has.

REFLECTION

1. Are there any relationships where you know you need to put on forgiveness or patience at the moment? How will you do that?

2. Who in your church needs your proactive and practical love at the moment?

DAY 18

READ Colossians 3:15–17

Paul has already made clear in verse 11 that the local church is to be centred around Jesus Christ – he 'is all, and is in all'. Everything about what we do and who we are as churches is about him. Here in these verses, Paul helps us to think about how Christ's presence shapes our church community.

Firstly, we see in verse 15 that *we're to build peace-filled churches*. He's already shown us the details of how Christ changes our relationships (see 3:8 and 12). Here we're reminded that the Prince of Peace lives amongst us and so, as his people, we should make every effort to be at peace with one another. We belong to him and to one another, and so divisiveness is always anti-Jesus.

Secondly, we see in verse 16 that *we're to build word-shaped churches*. The local church isn't a club or social work office, but a gathering of Christ's people around his word. We're defined by the gospel of Jesus Christ in all that we do – both inside the church and outside the church. We're not to be stingy with this gospel either, but 'rich' with it. We're all to overflow with it, teach it to one another (note this does not apply just to the pastor/minister/vicar!) and let it shape the kind of songs we sing.

Thirdly, *we're called to build thankful churches*. Three times thanksgiving is mentioned in these verses. We're not to be like the grumbling people of God in the wilderness, but to recognise God's incredible daily generosity to us through Jesus Christ. We have much to thank God for – everything that isn't hell in our lives is grace. If we see that, we'll become thankful churches.

By way of summary, Paul says that we're called to honour Christ in all we do (v. 17). Our lives individually, and together as his people, are about him. We're to build churches where the name of Christ is over everything we do. He is all for us.

REFLECTION

1. How can you help to build a local church that looks like this?

2. List the things you can give God thanks for today!

3. How is Christ's name honoured in your life at the moment?

DAY 19

READ Colossians 3:18–21

Here we have directions for how families are to be ordered under Christ's rule. These directions are given in the context of the new life in Christ spoken about in 3:1–4. Our families aren't abstracted from Christ, but they, too, come under his lordship and are shaped by his rule and power (see 3:17). This is why Paul talks, in the context of the family, about doing what is 'fitting in the Lord' (v. 18) and 'pleases the Lord' (v. 20).

Christ's pattern for husbands, according to verse 19, is that they exercise loving and gentle leadership. This loving leadership isn't about buying chocolates and flowers, but has already been given content by verses 12–13. It's about practising compassion, humility, kindness and forgiveness in the details of the marriage relationship. For wives, Christ's pattern is humble submission to their husband's loving leadership. Biblically speaking, submission is neither negative nor outdated, nor disrespectful of people's rights, but key to holiness. It's something practised by all believers in different areas (Eph. 5:21), and ultimately it's practised by Christ himself (John 5:19).

Life in Christ impacts parenting as well. Children aren't simply to give in to their parents or else to try to negotiate with them, but to obey (v. 20). Their obedience is meant to be full and complete 'in everything' and done willingly – echoing their obedience to Christ himself. Learning to obey parents is key for children learning to obey Christ himself. Fathers (whose role is to take a lead in discipline) are called to be gentle with their children, avoiding unnecessary confrontation, harsh rules and dictatorial leadership (v. 21). Their approach to their children is to be encouraging and strengthening rather than critical and nitpicking.

Lastly, notice what Paul doesn't say here about marriage and parenting. There are lots of things he doesn't prescribe or comment on, and many details are left out. God, in his wisdom, has given us some principles, but otherwise there is great freedom in how we order our marriages and family life.

REFLECTION

1. If you're married and/or have kids, where are you challenged by these verses? If you're not married/don't have kids, how can you support other believers in living these things out?

2. In what areas do believers have freedom in how to order their marriages/ families?

DAY 20

READ Colossians 3:22 – 4:1

In this section, Paul has been outlining the way that life in Christ shapes various relationships. Now he comes to slaves and slave owners. Slavery was very common in the ancient world, but it wasn't the same kind of institution as the African slave trade that we normally think of – generally it was more varied and allowed for greater freedoms. The challenge for the believers in the early church was that if, as Paul argued, background and social status no longer mattered in Christ, what did that mean for slaves and slave owners? Should slaves revolt? Should slavery be abolished? Paul's simple response is Christ-centred. His concern is that we live for Christ in the situation we're in. He is more concerned about sanctification than social revolution (though there's much here that implicitly undermines slavery as an institution – see Philemon).

Accordingly, Paul looks at the slave–slave owner relationship through the lens of being in Christ. For instance, he tells the Christian slaves to be the very best slaves they can be (v. 23). They shouldn't take advantage of their new status in Christ to avoid serving. Rather, they're to obey 'in everything' (v. 22). And yet even outward obedience isn't enough – it needs to be motivated by fear of the Lord and not just by seeking rewards from earthly masters. In reality, the slave is working for Christ, not their earthly master, and so their mind should be on the final inheritance coming on the last day (v. 24). Then, in 4:1 the slave owners are commanded to be just and fair in their treatment and not to misuse their power. Radically, here they're told that they themselves are slaves with a 'Master in heaven'. They'll have to give an account of themselves to him.

Whenever we find ourselves under authority, or with authority, such as in employee–employer or student–teacher relationships, we should always look at these relationships through Christ. The key question is always how we live for Christ in that relationship.

REFLECTION

1. Why is Paul concerned about the slaves' motivation here? How does motivation matter in what we do?

2. What does just and fair treatment (4:1, ESV) look like? How can you make sure you're doing that when you have authority over people?

DAY 21

READ Colossians 4:2–4

What kind of prayer life should we be aspiring to, as churches and individuals? Verse 2 gives us some clear instructions: 'Continue steadfastly in prayer, being watchful in it with thanksgiving' (ESV). Firstly, we are to continue in prayer. We are to cultivate prayerfulness; that is, ongoing habits of prayer. Secondly, we're called to be steadfast in prayer. We're to be immovable and unwavering in our prayerfulness. Keeping going in prayer when we 'don't feel like it' or when 'life is busy' is key to developing prayerfulness. Thirdly, Paul asks us to be watchful. This has the sense of being awake and alert to threat (Mark 14:37–38) or to the return of Christ (Luke 21:34–36). There's something we can do about spiritual dozing and lethargy; we can keep ourselves alert in prayer! On a very practical note, seek to develop habits of prayer that keep you awake (like speaking aloud and walking around) and don't entice you to sleep (such as sitting in a cosy armchair early in the morning with your eyes closed). Lastly, we're called to thankfulness (see 3:15–17). It's incredibly refreshing and encouraging to regularly list up, in prayer, the blessings we've received. Don't neglect it!

Paul is very aware himself of how dependent his ministry is on the prayerfulness of the local church (vv. 3–4). He needs 'open doors' for gospel proclamation and he needs clarity in that proclamation. These will come, he thinks, through the church's prayer. Prayer for missionaries and world mission should, therefore, also infuse all our praying because this is God's means of empowering them to do what he's sent them to do. They need us to pray. As we do that, we will reap spiritual benefits ourselves through a greater liberation from selfishness and a bigger vision of the glory of Christ amongst the nations (1:3–6).

REFLECTION

1. Where do you need to grow in your prayer life? How can you do that?

2. Are there any ways you could plan to pray for missionaries or world mission? How do you think praying for world mission would affect your spiritual life?

DAY 22

READ Colossians 4:5–6

Most believers spend large amounts of time with people who don't believe in Christ, and so these verses about how we're to live amongst outsiders are immediately relevant for our day-to-day lives. These verses come right after Paul has been speaking of his mission to declare Christ (4:3) – with the point being that believers are also called to declare Christ.

Firstly, we're commanded to 'Be wise' (v. 5). We've already learnt in Colossians that wisdom is summed up in Christ (2:3), and in 1:9–10 Paul prays that the Colossians might have wisdom to live lives worthy of Christ. Being wise towards outsiders, therefore, involves putting Christ on display as we live for him. By way of contrast, living foolishly would mean to 'hide' Christ and live without him. Never underestimate the wisdom that you have to share with the world around you! Furthermore, we should understand the urgency of this. We live in a time when God is waiting patiently for unbelievers to repent, not wanting anyone to perish (2 Pet. 3:9). Therefore, as Paul says at the end of verse 5, we should make good use of this opportunity or time to put Christ on display in our lives.

Secondly, we're to think, in particular, about our words. 'Conversation' here (v. 6) is exactly the same term translated as 'message' (or 'word', ESV) in verse 3. There is, therefore, most likely a connection between the 'word' Paul is wanting to declare, and the 'word' that is to come out of our mouths while we are amongst unbelievers. This 'word' that we share is to be full of grace and distinctiveness ('seasoned with salt'). Our speech is, as with the rest of life, to be filled with the new life of Christ in us. Our words are to be shaped by the gospel word so that we reflect Christ in small and big ways. People will have questions and objections, but our words, when shaped by the gospel word, will give answers.

This is the day that Christ has given you to live amongst outsiders. How will you make him known?

REFLECTION

1. How can outsiders see the wisdom of your life today? What will draw them to Christ through you?

2. What do you spend your time talking about? How much is it filled with the good things of Christ?

DAY 23

READ Colossians 4:7–9

The end of Paul's letter is the kind of passage that we may be tempted to 'skip over', as it might seem that it's just a series of references to people and greetings. This would be a mistake as God has also inspired this part of Colossians, and so we trust that there's much here to instruct us as well! We learn in these verses about Paul's fellow gospel workers who are being sent to Colossae by Paul.

First of all we meet Tychicus, who comes highly recommended and had been sent to encourage the Colossians (presumably also by delivering Paul's letter to them). Tychicus is described in verse 7 as a:

- 'dear brother' – gospel workers aren't meant to be rivals, nor professionals, but a network of brothers and sisters working together in love for each other.
- 'faithful minister' – starting spectacularly well isn't an indication that a leader will finish well. Faithfulness is the characteristic of ministry that comes through time and testing. Tychicus proved this in the long term – staying faithful with Paul to the end of his ministry (see 2 Tim. 4:12).
- 'fellow-servant' – as mentioned before, the word 'servant' is probably better translated as 'slave'. Paul and his team of gospel workers didn't see themselves as celebrity speakers but as people owned by a Master.

Secondly, we meet Onesimus. He isn't described as a minister, but as a brother (v. 9). The congregation would have known Onesimus as he was 'one of you' (v. 9). Notice, though, that Onesimus, despite being a slave (see Philemon), is treated by Paul in the same way as his own associates in ministry – and is, more importantly, described as a dearly loved and faithful brother. Here we see the radical effects of the gospel on relationships and social status (see 3:11 and 3:22 – 4:1). The marginalised and disregarded become our brother and sister in Christ. Being converted to Christ changes everything about who we are.

REFLECTION

1. What material does this passage give you for prayer for your spiritual leaders?

2. Are there believers in your context who you might not treat as dearly loved brothers and sisters? How might you change that?

DAY 24

READ Colossians 4:10–18

There's something deep in us that looks for heroes to follow. Mentors and role models have a massive influence on our choices and character, even if we're not always conscious of who they are.

Aristarchus (v. 10), in particular, shows us the radical commitment of discipleship. He's in prison with Paul at that moment for his ministry for Christ. Mark (v. 10) shows us the power of Christian reconciliation. He had at one point fallen out with Paul (see Acts 15:37–39), but he's now commended by Paul – and even described as a comfort to him (v. 11). Nympha (v. 15), most likely a woman of means, who hosted the local church in her home, shows us the importance of generosity and hospitality.

By way of contrast, though there are also some warnings for us in these verses. Demas (v. 14) proved unfaithful in the end (2 Tim. 4:10), hence the importance of faithfulness (see 1:7 and 4:7). Archippus (v. 17) was also in danger of not holding out in his service of Christ. Long-term perseverance is a key quality to look for in role models.

From Epaphras (v. 12 – and already mentioned in 1:7–8) we learn, firstly, how to pray. He constantly 'wrestles' in prayer (literally, 'agonising') for the church. Don't give up wrestling with God in this way on behalf of your local church. Secondly, we learn what to pray for. It's very easy for us to be diverted in prayer towards all kinds of goals and purposes, but his prayer is focused on God's priorities for the church (see 1:28–29): maturity and assurance. Lastly, we learn about working hard for the local church (v. 13). How easily we give our effort and energy to career, studies, hobbies and home improvement – but the local church deserves our very best work.

At the end, Paul himself reminds us of his own imprisonment as he writes this letter. It's striking to think that most of the New Testament wasn't written from an office or a quiet study, but from prison. Let Paul's willingness to suffer shape the kind of Christianity you want to live out in your life.

REFLECTION

1. Which one of these heroes struck you the most? Why? What can you learn from them?

2. Which heroes do you have in your life generally? How have they modelled Christ-like character to you?

MORE IN THIS SERIES

ROMANS
Momentous News
By David Cook
ISBN: 978-1-906173-24-1

MARK
The Suffering Servant
By Jeremy McQuoid
ISBN: 978-1-906173-55-5

DANIEL
Far From Home
By Justin Mote
ISBN: 978-1-906173-68-5

1 THESSALONIANS
Living for Jesus
By Julia Marsden
ISBN: 978-1-906173-67-8

PHILIPPIANS
Press Towards the Goal
By Kay Mumford
ISBN: 978-1-909611-31-3

GALATIANS
The Life I Now Live
By Peter Mead
ISBN: 978-1-910587-09-6

ACTS
To the Ends of the Earth
By David Cook
ISBN: 978-1-909611-02-3

EZEKIEL
For His Glory
By Peter Lau
ISBN: 978-1-909611-83-2

JOHN
Never Thirst Again
By David Cook
ISBN: 978-1-909611-30-6

and more at... 10 Publishing
a division of 10ofthose.com

To place an order call: **0330 2233 423** email: **sales@10ofthose.com**
or order online: **www.10ofthose.com**

Andy Mason
COLOSSIANS
ALIVE IN CHRIST